Quotes created with www.kittl.com

BRAIN
DELIGHT

If you THINK missing me is HARD then you SHOULD try missing YOU

If it's easy
EVERYONE
WOULD HAVE
DONE IT

You don't cross my heart
You live in it

SORRY
it's too late
to
quit

You're the only Reason I keep checking Flight ticket prices

Distance is a test
not a
problem

You are my favorite notification

DISTANCE
CAN
SUCK
IT

you ruin my day because you're not in it

I LOVE YOU
....
THE DOTS ARE THE LOVE
THAT IS STILL LOADING
AND I'LL TAKE
FOREVER
TO COMPLETE

I miss YOU
LIKE AN
IDIOT MISSES
THE
POINT

Suddenly
all love songs
ARE ABOUT YOU

I just want to rip you out of
MY DREAMS
and
HUG YOU

Send yourself please to me
I'll take care of the bees

I wish I could
copy paste you
into my bed

Together
We
can

You're
my favorite
HELLO
and my
hardest
GOODBYE

i've found
the
best
PERSON
in
the
WORLD
WHAT
possibly
could
BE
HARDER

You Are
miss
able
which
makes
my life
miserable

Stay out of my dreams
I just want ONE second without thinking about YOU

I got
A whole
Zoo in my stomach
thinking about you
not just butterflies

YOUR ABSENCE
is stronger
THAN SOME
PEOPLE'S PRESENCE

Sometimes
I MISS
you
That I
get Jealous
for no
Reason

It's
FUNNY
how you can
make me SMILE
while being
Away

Hell is distance
between
two people
who love
each other

FLOWERS ARE RED
The sky
is blue
YOU CAN'T
Imagine
HOW MUCH
I miss you

Made in the USA
Monee, IL
20 April 2024

57265818R00031